SAFER MOTORWAY DRIVING

GORDON COLE

LONDON

IAN ALLAN LTD

Contents

First published 1990

ISBN 0 7110 1964 9

Published by Ian Allan Ltd,
Shepperton, Surrey; and printed
by Ian Allan Printing Ltd at their
works at Coombelands in
Runnymede, England

Preface

Highway transportation is a vital factor in the economic and social life of a country. This is particularly true of motorways – truly the arteries of the land – for without them millions of vehicles would grind to a halt in the chaos of our already overcrowded roads.

Motorways have numerous advantages: the drivers who use them enjoy safer travel and greatly reduced journey times; cities and industries located near motorways benefit from faster and better communications with the outside world, which in turn brings in more trade and prosperity.

The worldwide network of motorways used today has taken decades to develop and construct. Italy was one of the first countries to construct roads for the exclusive use of motor traffic – in 1924 the Milan-Varese Autostrada was opened. A further section of 330 miles opened in the next 10 years. Germany, by the end of 1937, had opened almost 1,000 miles of Autobahnen and was in the process of constructing 1,100 more. In 1925 across the Atlantic the USA had completed its first 15½ miles of motorway – the Bronx River Parkway.

Holland had 70 miles of motorway by the start of World War 2 and by the end of the 1950s, Belgium had some 75 miles constructed and in use.

The first motorway in Sweden was opened in 1953. Denmark followed suit in 1957 and Norway in 1965. By the same year Austria had 190 miles of motorway complete: and Switzerland had constructed its first length of motorway in 1960.

The first motorway in the United Kingdom was the eight-mile Preston bypass which was officially opened in 1958. The UK was lagging behind many European countries in constructing motorways, but since 1960 successive governments have realised the importance and essential need for motorways and major construction has taken place throughout the British Isles.

Today motorways are the arteries of the world's land transport systems carrying commuters and cargo, private and public users. It is surprising, therefore, that a new driver has no experience of them under tuition or before he passes his driving test.

Safer Motorway Driving is designed to give experienced drivers or first-time users an outline of how to drive safely on the fastest roads available to us today.

All the photography was by the author, at different times of the day and in different seasons, using the natural light available at the time. The intention is to give the reader an insight into all the different lighting and weather conditions that can be expected when driving on a motorway.

Gordon Cole
Stevenage, 1990

Acknowledgements

I would like to thank the following police forces for their cooperation; without it, the pictures could not have been taken. It was a pleasure having the assistance of the various traffic patrols; also invaluable was the assistance of many civil engineering companies.

Hertfordshire Constabulary
Thames Valley Police
Bedfordshire Police
Essex Police
Metropolitan Police
Surrey Constabulary
Tayside Police
Leicestershire Constabulary
Sir William Halcrow & Partners
John Mowlem Civil Engineers
James Drake, Surveyor
Automobile Association, for the use of their recovery vehicle
Vauxhall Motors Ltd (Luton), who sponsored this book in the interest of road safety
Department of Transport

Right:
Can you cope?

1 Before You Join the Motorway

The Carriageway

Below:
THREE-LANE MOTORWAY.
Motorway carriageways are made either of concrete or asphalt; both are distinguishable by their colour. This three-lane motorway has an asphalt road surface.

Restrictions

It was not until the Special Roads Act 1949 that legal powers were introduced to restrict motorways to the exclusive use of certain motor traffic. This Act legalised both the construction of special roads, and the conversion of existing roads into special roads, to which access would be restricted, and which could only be used by certain specified classes of traffic. The Act also gave the necessary powers to alter or close up any side roads, public footpaths or private accesses which crossed the route of the special road.

Motorways are dual-carriageway roads which must not be used by:

● Pedestrians
● Animals
● Learner drivers (except HGV)
● Pedal cycles
● Motorcycles under 50cc capacity
● Mopeds
● Slow moving vehicles carrying oversized loads (except by special permission)
● Agricultural vehicles
● Invalid carriages not exceeding 5cwt unladen weight
● Track-laying vehicles
● Vehicles not capable of attaining a speed of 25mph on the level when unladen and not drawing a trailer

Right:

ASPHALT CARRIAGEWAY.
This asphalt surface was hot-rolled when laid, with precoated chippings rolled into the surface to give a high resistance to skidding. However, the surface is impervious and this means that during a heavy shower, there could be standing water on the road surface, particularly if the gradient, as here, doesn't allow the rain water to dissipate. If you are driving a vehicle at 70mph with tyres whose tread depth is near the legal limit, they will not be adequate to disperse the water. The water that cannot be dispersed because of inadequate tread will be pushed forward, thereby inducing 'aquaplaning', when loss of vehicle control could be imminent.

Rain water usually disperses quickly, but water can cover a flat area — due to inadequate superelevation, and/or crossfall — and take a long time to drain away.

Right:

WATERLOGGED CARRIAGEWAY.
Too many drivers disregard adverse weather and drive too fast for the prevailing conditions. Maintaining an excessive speed in poor visibility caused by spray thrown up by heavy goods vehicles coupled with the density of rain, makes standing water difficult to detect, particularly at night.

Centre left:
CONCRETE CARRIAGEWAY.
You can tell concrete carriageways by colour. They also produce a distinctive noise when you drive on them. If you hear this, don't be concerned. It can vary in pitch and volume and is caused by the tyres, especially the radial type that have a steel bracing. Make sure your tyres comply with the law and are inflated to the correct pressure.

Above left:
CONCRETE ROAD.
After the surface of a concrete carriageway has been laid it is brushed in a transverse direction. This provides a satisfactory skid-resistant surface because the tyres are in contact with the peak of the brush finish and grooves assist drainage. Cracking in the carriageway is due to the many stresses involved.

Left:
WIDTH OF CARRIAGEWAYS.
On a dual two-lane motorway, the width of each lane is 3.60m. This measurement is taken from the outer edge line of the hard shoulder, to the outer edge of the lane line. The hard shoulder is 3.3m wide.

Right:
THREE-LANE CARRIAGEWAY.
On a dual three-lane motorway, the width of the nearside and middle lanes is 3.55m. These measurements are taken from the outer edge of the hard shoulder to the outer edge of the first lane line, then from the outer edge of the first lane line to the outer edge of the second lane line. The width of the outside lane is 3.50m. This measurement is taken from the outer edge of the lane line to the outer edge of the central reserve line. The nearside and middle lanes are wider than the outside lane, to assist the movement of heavy goods vehicles.

Below right:
FOUR-LANE CARRIAGEWAY.
On a four-lane dual carriageway, the width of the nearside and second lane is the same as that of the first and second lane of a dual three-lane motorway (3.55m). The third and fourth lanes are 3.50m wide. The measurements are taken from the outer edges of the lane line to that of the central reserve. On a motorway that has five lanes, the measurements would be similar to a four-lane carriageway.

Above:
HARD SHOULDER.
A motor vehicle, just like any other piece of machinery, will give efficient and reliable service provided it is well treated, well maintained and kept properly adjusted. This will also reduce the nuisance of involuntary stoppages and mechanical breakdowns. People don't always fully appreciate this fact. Many thousands of motorists use the Emergency telephones every day and put an unnecessary burden on the police information rooms which have to deal with these breakdowns and other kindred matters. Very few such calls are concerned directly with police matters; the bulk is initiated either by negligence or ignorance on the part of the motorists concerned.

Both for your own sake and that of other road users and pedestrians it is your responsibility as driver to make sure the roadworthiness of your vehicle is checked and complies with the law. This also applies to any load — its security and weight. Do this before the journey starts, otherwise you could commit an offence or be involved in a serious accident.

Left:
NO HARD SHOULDER.
There is no hard shoulder on this slip lane. If your vehicle breaks down in this sort of circumstance, move it as far to the left as possible and switch on the hazard warning lights. At night leave your side lights on as well. Do not open the doors nearest the carriageway and do not stand at the rear of the vehicle or between it and passing traffic.

Below left:
INFORMATION SIGN.
The information given by this traffic sign is clear. If your vehicle is showing signs of mechanical trouble, you should pull up on the existing hard shoulder and try to rectify the problem, or use an emergency telephone to summon assistance. If you keep going and hope, your vehicle could break down on the carriageway, and could thereby cause a dangerous obstruction, putting your own safety and that of others at risk.

Whenever a vehicle stops on the hard shoulder, it becomes a hazard and creates potential danger, not only to the driver and passenger(s) but also passing traffic. There are some drivers whose prime concern seems to be to find out why a vehicle has stopped, particularly when the police are present. Because of this they divert their attention to get a better look. Far too many accidents and traffic jams are caused this way. Don't do this — don't reduce speed to have a look and cause chaos.

Hard shoulders are provided on most motorways in the United Kingdom. They are provided for emergency use only, and should be used only if your vehicle breaks down: ie a mechanical/electrical failure and/or if a tyre is punctured. Hard shoulders are usually 3.3m wide. Some slip roads and deceleration lanes have no hard shoulders, so if your vehicle breaks down you should warn other drivers of the obstruction, by using the hazard lights if fitted or by using a red reflecting triangle.

The verges behind the hard shoulders accommodate drains, electricity, emergency telephone services, safety fences and signs.

Safety Factors

Right:
WHITE MARGINAL/RUMBLE STRIPS.
White marginal strips are provided at each edge of the carriageway. One strip is placed at the edge of the nearside carriageway and the other edge of the hard shoulder. The majority of marginal strips are dual purpose, being combined into rumble strips which are made from reflectorised paint and glass beads (ballontini). They define the edge of the carriageway, and therefore assist drivers to recognise it at night and in fog. Should you drive over a rumble strip unintentionally, you will feel a strong vibration on the steering.

Far right, top:
The other marginal strip is placed at the outer edge of the offside lane and the central reserve. This strip is also often combined into a rumble strip.

Far right, bottom:
LANE LINE MARKINGS.
White reflectorised paint is used for lane markings along the carriageway thereby assisting drivers to position their vehicles correctly, particularly during the hours of darkness and in fog. The lane markings are 2m long, with a 7m gap between them. White cats-eyes or studs are placed between every other lane marking.

Far left, top:

RED CATS-EYES (UNDIRECTIONAL).
The carriageway markings are defined further by reflective road studs called cats-eyes. There are red, green, white and amber cats-eyes. The red ones are placed at the nearside edge of the carriageway, 18m apart for general use and 9m apart when the main, slip and link roads have a radius less than 450m. They are also used where fog is prevalent; at the nearside edge of merge and diverge; and 3m apart at both sides of the edge of the hatching between a slip road and the carriageway.

Far left, bottom:

WHITE CATS-EYES (BIDIRECTIONAL).
White cats-eyes are placed 18m apart between every other white line on the main carriageway; 9m apart where fog is prevalent; 8m apart where carriageways diverge and 7.3m apart between lane markings on link roads where the radius is less than 450m.

Left:

AMBER STUDS (BIDIRECTIONAL).
Amber studs are placed at the offside of the carriageway 18m apart and 9m staggered from the red and white cats-eyes. They are 9m apart where the radius is less than 450m on a main carriageway, on slip and link roads, and where fog is prevalent.

Right:

**GREEN CATS-EYES
(UNDIRECTIONAL).**
Green cats-eyes are placed
across merging/diverging
tapers at standard junctions
(entrances to and exits from
slip roads).

Centre right:

**GREEN STUDS
(TEMPORARY).**
Temporary green studs are
placed on the carriageway
when extensive roadworks
are taking place. These studs
also have red reflecting
glasses that face oncoming
traffic to emphasise
potential danger.

Far right:

DIRECTION ARROWS.
White reflectorised direction
arrows are used in
conjunction with traffic
signs, where there is
considerable traffic
movement at an interchange,
or the interchange is
complex.

Right:

SAFETY BARRIER (CORRUGATED SHEET METAL). Various methods have been used to provide a safety barrier to prevent vehicles crossing the central reserve, or going down a steep embankment when out of control. They include steel guard rails, wire ropes and dense shrubs, but no ideal method has been found. If a barrier is too rigid, vehicles rebound back on to the carriageway into the path of following vehicles. This barrier is made of corrugated sheet steel.

The minimum height of a safety barrier is 580mm; the maximum 640mm. A continuous safety barrier is provided on the central reserve and other locations, for example when the motorway is on an embankment with a 20ft or more drop to either side; on the outer verge of embankments 10ft or more high; where the radius of a curve is 2,800ft or less; and at the approaches to all bridges and at any point of potential danger.

Far right, top:

SAFETY BARRIER. This photograph illustrates well the use of safety barriers to stop vehicles leaving the carriageway and going down a steep embankment.

Far right, bottom:

METAL OPEN BOX BARRIER. This metal open box safety barrier is at the start of a slip lane and should prevent a vehicle going down a steep embankment and on to the motorway.

Far left:

FRENCH DRAINS.
An effective drainage system is essential on a motorway, to prevent dangerous ponding of water on the carriageways in heavy rain. If the carriageway is waterlogged, don't drive at too high a speed; you could easily lose control.

One of the main types of drainage on motorways is called a 'French drain'. Situated on the central reserve (as here) or on the verge beside the hard shoulder, a French drain consists of an open-jointed or porous pipe laid in a trench about 1m deep. This is then filled with loose stones, forming a filter through which water can percolate on its way to the main water-course.

Above left:

FRENCH DRAIN (NEARSIDE).
Don't drive on a French drain at the edge of the hard shoulder because your wheels might sink.

Left:

OILTRAPS.
Water from the carriageways filters through the French drains to an oiltrap. This does exactly what its name suggests — collects any oil washed from the carriageway before the water passes to the outfall and into the rivers. This complies with the river authorities' requirements both for reduction of pollution and also because the storage pond controls the flow of water into the watercourses, thus preventing flooding.

Below right:
BREAKDOWNS.
A vehicle has broken down in the nearside lane. Instead of making some effort to warn approaching traffic of the obstruction, the driver and passenger are standing on the carriageway with their backs facing any approaching traffic, discussing what their next move should be.

Far right, top:
The passenger decides that he will go to the emergency telephone, and takes his dog for company. The dog is not on a lead.

Far right, bottom:
The driver has become bored waiting, and has decided to join his friend, thus leaving the vehicle unattended and on the carriageway. No effort has been made to remove the vehicle to the hard shoulder, or to warn approaching traffic of the danger of the obstruction.
   It may seem unlikely, but this sort of thing happens every day.

Motorway Regulations

The Highway Code gives sound, commonsense advice about what a driver should do while driving on a motorway. Failure to take heed of such advice has caused many deaths and serious injuries. The following pictures show dangerous situations created by irresponsible drivers. These situations have actually occurred, and have led to serious injury or death — both to the drivers who committed the offences and innocent people.

Far left:

STOPPING ON THE CARRIAGEWAY — 1.
It is an offence to stop on the carriageway for any reason, unless you are requested to do so by the Police, a traffic signal or a cause beyond your control. This driver has stopped on the carriageway to look at a map, in doing so he has committed an offence and created a dangerous situation.

Left:

STOPPING ON THE CARRIAGEWAY — 2.
This driver has decided to stop in a gap in the central reserve. Apart from sudden mechanical failure, there is no reason why the driver should stop in such a potentially dangerous place.

Below left:

STOPPING ON THE CARRIAGEWAY — 3.
The driver of this vehicle has created a potentially lethal situation. The vehicle has developed mechanical failure while in the outside lane. Action should be taken to warn approaching traffic of the obstruction immediately — either by using the hazard warning lights (providing the fault is not an electrical one) or by placing a red reflecting triangle at the rear of the vehicle. Time, weather, lighting conditions and volume of traffic on the motorway at the time are factors that decide what action should be taken first. This driver has decided to use the emergency telephone, when another driver could have assisted him.

Right:

STOPPING ON THE CARRIAGEWAY — 4.
This driver has stopped on the carriageway because a vehicle in front has made a late decision to leave the motorway. Many people stop dead from sheer panic, the cause of numerous accidents. Do not stop on the motorway unless forced to.

Far right:

U-TURNS.
The action being taken by this driver — making a right turn across the gap in the central reserve — is completely irresponsible. This manoeuvre has been the cause of numerous fatal accidents. Should you realise that you are travelling in the wrong direction, there is no alternative but to continue on to the next junction and change direction there. The gaps in the central reserve are emergency crossing points and are currently being blocked by safety barriers, thereby preventing drivers from making this lethal manoeuvre.

Right:

This driver has realised that he has travelled too far and has decided to make a 'U' turn on the carriageway for an exit in the distance. This dangerous manoeuvre has happened more often than you'd expect. It is, obviously, illegal and dangerous.

Left:
**REVERSING.
This driver is about to pass
his exit. Instead of
continuing on to the next
exit, he has decided to stop
on the carriageway and
reverse. Numerous dangers
are created by this. If you
realise that you have just
passed the exit you should
have used, there is no choice
but to continue on to the next
exit, regardless of distance.**

Far left, bottom:
**Motorways are dual
carriageways. How anyone
should get confused with
which way the traffic flows
or how to join a motorway is
surprising.**

Below left:
**Should your vehicle run out
of petrol, you should use the
emergency telephone to seek
assistance, and not walk
along the hard shoulder to
the next exit, as these two
people are doing.**

Right:

PROHIBITED TRAFFIC — 1.
Cyclists are prohibited to use motorways but some do. In doing so they create danger for themselves and others.

Far right:

PROHIBITED TRAFFIC — 2.
Agricultural vehicles are not allowed to use a motorway. This one did and suffered mechanical breakdown. The driver has since appeared in court.

Below right:

PROHIBITED TRAFFIC — 3.
A pedestrian can be seen on the hard shoulder trying to hitch a lift; in doing so he is committing an offence and so too would any driver who stopped to offer him a lift. It is an offence to stop on a motorway when there is no emergency.

2 Approaching and Joining a Motorway

Approaching a Motorway

A motorway can be joined either from its start — possibly as a continuation of a primary road — from a roundabout, a spur road or slip lane. Once the motorway sign has been passed, motorway regulations are in force.

Far left:
INTERNATIONAL MOTORWAY SIGN.
This is the international motorway sign. The letter M signifies that the road ahead is a motorway, and the number — here 90 — is the number of the motorway. Once you have passed the sign, motorway regulations must be complied with at all times. You will be guilty of an offence if you use a motorway when prohibited from doing so.

In the distance is a bridge across the motorway. The minimum bridge height on British motorways is 5.3m.

Left:
MOTORWAY SIGN.
This sign used to be placed at the start of every motorway in the United Kingdom. It shows which vehicles are prohibited to use the motorway. The sign has now been replaced by the international sign. To find which vehicles are excluded from motorways, look in the *Highway Code.*

Far left:

ADVISORY SIGNS.
Should you be travelling on a primary road which is about to lead into a motorway in a prohibited vehicle, you must continue on the primary road following advisory signs like this one.

Centre left:

ADVISORY SIGN.
This is another example of an advisory sign reminding road users that the road ahead leads on to a motorway. Anyone prohibited from using a motorway should make sure the spur road is not entered, otherwise they will be committing an offence.

Above left:

WARNING SIGN.
This warning sign is self-explanatory. Drivers must not drop passengers on the spur road; if this happens the driver and passenger(s) (who thus become pedestrian(s)) will commit an offence.

Left:

SPUR ROAD.
You will pass the international motorway sign as you join a spur road, and from that point on you must comply with motorway regulations. Some spur roads have a hard shoulder, others not. The driver seen parked on the hard shoulder is reading a map and in doing so is committing an offence. The hard shoulder is for emergency use only, and is not a safe place to plan a route. This should have been done well before reaching the motorway.

Right:

When the advisory sign has been passed, a driver/rider will see a direction sign. Should you need to change course for your intended direction of travel, don't forget to make effective use of your mirrors and make a direction indicator signal. Always bear in mind, however, that a signal only informs other road users of your intention. It does not give you right of way. A change of course should not be made unless it is safe to do so.

Below right:

You should plan your driving/riding well ahead so that you give yourself ample time to get into the appropriate lane. You should not drive over the white herringbone chevrons because of late positioning, impatience or inconsiderate driving. If you do, you will commit an offence.

Far right:

NO SERVICES ON MOTORWAY.

Not all motorways have service areas provided for drive-in stopping places, where commercial and private users are offered fuel, emergency repair, parking, cafeteria, restaurant and toilet facilities. It is therefore important that you consult a good up-to-date road map, so that any journey can be achieved free of problems and as comfortably as possible.

Joining a Motorway

Left:
MAXIMUM SPEED.
The maximum speed on a motorway is 70mph, provided it is safe to do so. There may be temporary maximum speed limit signs displayed on matrix warning signals that are situated on the central reservation, or on an overhead gantry sign. Should the matrix signals and/or overhead gantry signs be showing a speed limit lower than 70mph, amber lights will be seen flashing alternately above and below the legend (speed shown) to give warning and to draw drivers' attention to the legend shown.

Right:

SPEED RESTRICTION SIGN.
Sometimes approaching a motorway a warning signal will inform you that there is an advisory speed limit in operation (here 50mph). You should comply with this instruction.

Below right:

STOP SIGN.
Should you approach or be on a motorway when flashing red signals are shown, you must not go beyond them. You should make effective use of your mirror(s) and switch on your hazard warning lights, thereby warning any following traffic that you are about to reduce speed. This should be achieved by smooth application of the footbrake. You should stop your vehicle just before the red flashing signals, and wait until you are advised otherwise.

Sometimes the reason for the restriction shown by the signal may not be apparent but there may, for example, be an accident ahead or a belt of fog. It is essential for the Police to be able to restrict the movement of traffic well in advance of a given situation. Apart from being dangerous not to comply with flashing red signals, you will also be committing an offence.

Left:

DOUBLE ACCELERATION LANES.

As you reach the end of the slip road, it continues into an acceleration lane. This lane has been designed so that you can adjust your speed as the situation demands by accelerating, decelerating or braking to match the road speed of the traffic on the motorway. Effective use of mirrors is of the utmost importance. What can and cannot be seen in them will determine whether you can join the motorway or not. If there is a safe gap in the traffic in the left-hand lane, signal your intention to move out by using a direction indicator signal, then adjust your speed so that you join the motorway at the same speed as traffic in the left-hand lane. The use of an 'I intend to move out' direction indicator signal, gives you no right of way whatsoever. Some drivers think it does, and force their way on to the left or even second lane, and in doing so force drivers on the motorway to brake hard to avoid them. Numerous serious and fatal accidents have occurred because of this sort of inconsiderate and aggressive driving.

Left:

DOWNHILL SLIP ROAD.

The majority of slip roads and acceleration lanes on motorways in the United Kingdom are on a downhill gradient. This is to assist drivers to obtain the speed necessary to join the motorway.

Above:

DOUBLE SLIP ROAD.

Should you join a motorway that has a double slip road, you should try to get into the appropriate lane for your intended direction of travel as soon as possible. Should you have to move to another lane, you must make sure it is safe to change course before making the appropriate manoeuvre. Effective use of the mirrors should be made, so that you will be aware of the position and speed of any following traffic. A signal of intent should be given, and when safe to do so a change of course can be made. At the end of either slip road you will be in the acceleration lane.

Right:

PROCEEDING ON TO THE ACCELERATION LANE.
This driver is on a slip road and about to proceed on to the acceleration lane.

Far right:

SIGNAL OF INTENTION.
The driver has made effective use of the mirrors. A safe gap has been seen in the traffic on the left-hand lane of the motorway, and he is signalling his intention to move out, at the same time increasing his speed.

Below right:

BEING OVERTAKEN.
Should another driver overtake you while in the acceleration lane, let him/her get well past before you decide to join the motorway, as your view of the carriageway could be obscured by the overtaking vehicle.

Left:
WHITE HATCHING.
Areas of white hatching painted on the road are to separate traffic. Do not drive over a hatching that has a solid white edge line, except in an emergency, otherwise you will be committing an offence. If you drive over a hatching that has a broken white edge line, and in doing so collide with another vehicle, a charge of undue care and attention could be brought against you. This driver is trying to take a short cut on to the motorway by driving over hatching that has solid white edge lines; in doing so he is committing an offence.

Far left, bottom:
REVERSING ON SLIP ROAD.
Once you have entered a slip road you must continue on to the motorway unless traffic signs or Police direct you to do otherwise. It is an offence to reverse on a slip lane like this driver, regardless of the circumstances at the time.

Left:
ACCELERATION LANE.
The slip lane continues into the acceleration lane. If you join a motorway at a place where a link road from another motorway also joins, it may look complex and confusing. This traffic sign shows that the acceleration lane runs parallel with another acceleration lane from a link road. The sign also shows that you will join the motorway in a fourth lane that starts from the end of the acceleration lane. You should therefore stay in your lane.

Right:

LINK ROAD/ACCELERATION LANE.
Any traffic in the lane to your right will normally join the motorway before you do, as your acceleration lane continues on a little further. You must give way to traffic already on the motorway. Do not race with the vehicles from the link road to join the motorway first. If you do, you will create a dangerous situation. It is better to be late for an appointment than dead.

Below right:

HATCHING.
This driver is treating the hatching as a Give Way area. An offence is being committed and the action taken by the driver is dangerous, not only to himself and his passengers but numerous other drivers as well.

Left:
SIGNALS.
It cannot be stressed too much that use of a direction indicator gives you no right of way. Numerous drivers seem to misconstrue the true purpose of these signals. They charge down the acceleration lane not knowing if the nearside lane is clear, due to lack of rear observation. You should give way to traffic already on the motorway. If there isn't a suitable gap in the traffic, wait in the acceleration lane until it is safe to join the motorway. Be aware of the capabilities — particularly the power of acceleration — of the vehicle you are driving before deciding to join the motorway.

Left:
ON TO THE CARRIAGEWAY.
You should join the motorway in the left-hand lane. Do not cut across two or more lanes in one manoeuvre. This is dangerous and inconsiderate, and has been the cause of many serious accidents. Stay in the left-hand lane long enough to get used to the speed of traffic before trying to overtake.

3 On the Motorway

Below right:

After joining the motorway, stay in the left-hand lane long enough to get acclimatised to being on a motorway. Traffic travels faster on motorways compared with other roads, so it is very important that you are aware of the position and speed of following traffic. This can only be achieved by making effective use of the mirror(s) regularly.

Bottom right:

SEPARATION DISTANCE. One of the biggest causes of motorway accidents is the lack of separation (following) distance between vehicles. Many drivers are seen, day and night, driving too close to the vehicle in front with no margin for safety regardless of the weather conditions, and the volume and speed of traffic. This foolhardy attitude is based on the misapprehension that the vehicle in front cannot stop dead. If the car in front does stop dead and you are following it too closely, you will hit it. You should always allow the minimum stopping distance as shown in the *Highway Code*, between you and the vehicle in front.

Far left:
There are thousands of drivers who wish they had complied with the advice given on this traffic sign. Because they didn't a serious or a fatal accident took place. Always allow yourself a safe following distance from the vehicle in front, this being at least 1m for every mile per hour, thus 60mph = 60m from the vehicle in front on a dry road. This figure should be doubled if the road surface is wet, and trebled when ice and snow are present.

Left:
Always look well ahead; you will be able then to anticipate the actions of other drivers — unlike the two drivers illustrated. The driver on the left can be seen on the acceleration lane. He obviously thinks he has the right of way to emerge on to the carriageway. In fact, the driver on the carriageway has the right of way, but should they both continue on their present course an accident would occur. The driver on the carriageway is taking evasive action by braking and in doing so will prevent an accident.

Left:
Driving for long distances may make you feel drowsy. To prevent this, you should make sure there is plenty of fresh air in your vehicle. But be careful; if you open the windows when the wind is gusty it could affect the stability and handling of the vehicle. If the weather is like this, reduce speed.

Right:
Proper and adequate use of the mirror(s) cannot be emphasised enough.

Below right:
It is obvious that this minibus is going to join the motorway despite its lack of signal of intention. The driver behind should now use the mirror(s) and consider reducing speed.

Far right, top:
The driver of the minibus has finally decided to give a signal of intent far too late to be of any use. The driver behind has slowed to let him join the motorway.
Regardless of whether you have the right of way in a given situation, it is always safer to reduce speed slightly and let the inconsiderate driver have the right of way, rather than continue and collide with the vehicle in question!

Far right, bottom:
When you see a car in an acceleration lane on your left, you should ask yourself: 'Has the driver seen me? Will he pull out in front of me? What is behind me? Is it safe to reduce speed or move to another lane?'
  We know vehicles on the carriageway have the right of way, but a lot of drivers are not aware of this rule. Always plan your driving well ahead.

Left:
Not all motorways have service areas and so signs like this remind you that, should fuel or some other facility be required, you will have to leave the motorway at the next exit and find the appropriate service.

Should a driver allow his vehicle to run out of fuel, a number of problems can arise — not only the inconvenience or financial problems, but the safety of the vehicle and its occupants can be at risk. This situation can be aggravated during the hours of darkness. Always make sure your vehicle has adequate fuel on board to complete the intended journey, or that you can reach a service station.

No Services
on Motorway

Direction Signs

A national system of traffic signs has been designed for motorways so that they can be easily read by drivers travelling at speed. They are placed at the start of the motorway, on the verge next to the hard shoulder, over the carriageway (especially where there is considerable traffic movement, like heavy goods vehicles on the approach to an interchange) and/or when an interchange is complex. Overhead gantry signs are used to direct traffic into the correct lane well in advance of an interchange. Other signs are placed either one mile or half a mile from an exit. At some junctions the number of lanes is reduced; at others there is an increase. Signs show the lane that you should be in for your desired destination, and some indicate that traffic could join the carriageway on the nearside. Most of the signs have blue backgrounds and are rectangular in shape.

Below right:
This sign informs a driver that there is an intersection ahead, the number of the junction being 21A. When you plan a journey, use the number of the exit required as the reference point rather than the town or road number shown on the sign. This can save confusion if more than one exit serves the location you want. You must not look at a map while you are driving; doing this has often resulted in accidents.

Should a driver not wish to go on the M1 south or the A405, he should take immediate steps to make sure it is safe to change course to the present middle lane. This can only be achieved by making effective use of the mirror(s), and when safe to do so give an 'I intend to move out to the right' direction indicator signal. The mirrors should be used again, and if still safe to do so, a change in course can be made.

Above right:
This sign informs a driver that the left lane is designated for traffic whose intention is to go on the M1 south or the A405. The intersection is about 400yd away and you should be able to move into the middle lane in time if you need it.

Far left:

An overhead gantry sign can be seen after the last sign. White arrows are also used to assist drivers during the hours of darkness.

Above left:

This sign is one mile from the exit to which it refers. No town names are seen on the sign, but the exit number is given. If you want to leave the motorway at this exit, and should there be a lot of traffic on the motorway, then try to get into the left lane at the one mile distance sign. Don't try to leave a motorway from the second or third lane at the last minute when the actual slip road is seen. This dangerous action has been the cause of many accidents.

Left:

This sign is the follow-on sign from the previous one, half a mile from the next exit. The other difference is that it carries the name of the main town fed by the A43. At this half-mile distance, you should have already used your mirrors so that you are aware of the position and speed of any following traffic.

Right:

A self-explanatory sign giving advance warning of motorways merging.

Centre right:

This sign informs you that an additional lane has been provided, so that the motorway can be joined without causing any disruption to traffic already on the motorway.

Below right:

Drivers who are travelling on the motorway should see this sign, informing them that traffic could be joining the carriageway on their left.

Far right:

The information given on the sign can be clearly seen. Always make sure it is safe to change course before you do so.

Below right:
This sign warns a driver that traffic merges from the left with equal priority. The sign should be seen while travelling on the primary carriageway, and before reaching the motorway that is about to merge. On seeing the sign, you should use your mirror(s), so that you are aware of the speed and position of any following traffic. You should also look towards the merging motorway, in case a driver does not comply with the road markings.

Bottom right:
A straightforward warning sign which, combined with the view of the terrain ahead, makes it obvious that the instruction should be complied with.

Far right, top:
Some motorways pass close to an airfield, either civilian or military; warning signs like this inform drivers of the possibility that low-flying aircraft or sudden aircraft noise could occur.

Warning Signs

The majority of signs used on motorways have blue backgrounds and are rectangular in shape. However, there are some situations that justify a warning sign, thereby informing drivers of potential danger. Most of the warning signs shown here can be seen in the *Highway Code*.

Left:
This sign gives a warning that there is an uphill gradient ahead. There is no crawler lane, therefore drivers should anticipate seeing slow-moving heavy goods vehicles negotiating the incline.

Below left:
PROHIBITORY SIGN. Entry to a motorway maintenance compound by unauthorised persons is prohibited. Many dangers can arise from the movement of heavy plant in the compound.

Below right:
On some very busy motorways, the signals are overhead, one signal for each lane. This gantry sign has a dual purpose: it is a direction sign and signal.

Bottom right:
The matrix signal is showing a temporary maximum speed of 60mph. The speed limit applies to all lanes, and should be complied with.

Far right:
An accident has occurred further on, therefore it is imperative for safety reasons that the Police apply a temporary maximum speed limit. The signals can be seen on a gantry sign and then again at an intersection. It only takes one incident on a motorway to cause a backlog of traffic like this.

Special Signals

Special signals are often used on motorways — usually they are of the dot matrix type. In normal conditions they are blank. In dangerous conditions, or when the Police think it necessary to reduce the speed or even stop traffic, special signals will be seen illuminated on the roadside or above the carriageway on a gantry.

Left:
At the end of a restriction you should see a signal. There are two types. The information shown on the matrix signal informs you that the temporary speed limit is lifted and the national speed limit applies.

Below left:
Here the matrix signal has the word 'END' displayed.

Information Signs

The information signs to be seen on motorways differ in size, shape and colour. Some inform and some warn. The following are examples of the types and the information they give.

Below right:

This sign has been placed on a slip road and informs you that motorway regulations still apply. If you drop passengers you will be committing an offence.

Bottom right:

This sign has been placed on the approach to where roadworks are being carried out. It warns the driver of a vehicle 3m or more in width, that he must report to the Police at the place shown, so that assistance through the roadworks can be given.

Far right, top:

Tourist attraction signs are usually on a brown background and indicate the best route to the intended location.

Far right, bottom:

Make regular stops if you are travelling long distances, a sensible length of time being after two hours' driving. Even if you don't take refreshment you should park, secure the vehicle, and take a walk as exercise. Too many drivers try to drive too far without a break and in consequence, lack concentration either through tiredness or inadequate vehicle ventilation. This has been the cause of many serious and fatal accidents. This sign informs a driver that there are two service areas ahead.

Above:

To assist drivers to plan their travel, local radio stations broadcast frequent information regarding traffic congestion. Just tune in to the wavelengths listed on the sign.

Above right:

The sign indicates that the River Soar passes underneath the motorway. This sign is used as a point of reference, and not for drivers to stop and look at the view!

Right:

This sign informs a driver that if the intended destination is East Anglia, the A12 should be joined at the appropriate intersection.

Speed Limits

Contrary to popular belief, the design of motorways has been based on a minimum visibility distance, both horizontally and vertically, at 70mph. Visibility on the majority of motorways is good, but in isolated cases, speeds above 70mph could be dangerous in an emergency.

On some motorways there are curves but no bends. Due to the higher speed that traffic travels on motorways compared with other types of road, it is essential that a driver has a good view of the road ahead — the 'sight distance'. This is the clear distance over which a driver, entering a curve, is able to see an obstruction from an assumed eye level of 3ft 6in above the surface of the road. The minimum sight distance required along a motorway is 295m (950ft), in both vertical and horizontal planes. This sight distance is equivalent to the minimum stopping distance for a speed of 70mph while travelling round a curve. A vehicle travelling at 70mph would cover a distance of 950ft in 9sec. Remember that smooth hard-wearing road surfaces are provided on motorways, but these may have a very low coefficient of friction when wet. In adverse weather conditions, the stopping distance should be doubled.

After travelling some distance on a motorway, there is a tendency for a driver to increase speed without being aware of the fact. Long straight stretches can have a hypnotic and monotonous effect, and what is called parallelism can affect a

driver, especially when tired. This is why motorways have curves, to prevent parallelism and help the driver to remain alert. Considering the preliminary alignment of the route, the design layout of a motorway supplied by the surveyor has to incorporate the significance of sight distance in relation to the curvature, bridges and other fixtures that could obstruct a driver's view, with economies in mind. It is unlikely therefore that motorway speed limits will ever change much.

Right:
**When extensive carriageway
repairs are being undertaken,
it is necessary to have a
reduced speed limit.
Remember when
approaching roadworks, that
workmen have to repair the
carriageway. While doing so,
vehicles pass within a few
feet of them, at speeds far
outside the bounds of safety
for the prevailing conditions.
Because of the disregard for
the workmen's safety, a
compulsory reduced speed
limit had to be introduced. If
the temporary mandatory
speed limit is not complied
with, a driver could be
prosecuted.**

Breakdowns

Breakdowns — caused by mechanical or electrical problems or a punctured tyre — create numerous safety problems on a motorway. A driver has a great deal to think about, when a breakdown occurs. Should it happen while driving in the second or third lane, the surrounding traffic situation must be taken into account, ie the position and speed of vehicles on the left and to the rear. Providing the fault is not electrical, an 'I intend to move in to the left' direction indicator signal should be used and the side lights switched on, to supplement a stop-light signal. Do not use the brakes at this stage (unless of course the traffic ahead of you is slowing down). If the engine is about to, or has already stopped, the clutch pedal should be pressed down and the gear lever moved into neutral position, thereby maintaining

the road speed of the vehicle. You will need this to move towards the hard shoulder. A reduction of speed will have occurred by now, and it should be obvious to other road users that your intention is to get to the hard shoulder, but this assumption should not be taken for granted.

You should look over your left shoulder, to make sure that the driver on your nearside is going to allow you to move over on to the hard shoulder. The vehicle should be brought to rest as close as possible to the verge, but not on to a French drain. The handbrake must be applied (on), the ignition switched off and if possible switch the hazard warning lights on. Always react quickly with the first sign of mechanical, electrical or tyre problems. You should take the required action to reach the hard shoulder, preferably near an emergency telephone, thereby reducing the risk of other potential dangers.

Below, far left:
To help you find the nearest emergency telephone, special marker posts are placed on the verge next to the hard shoulder. They are predominantly white with a red reflective strip on the front.

Below left:
The road faces of the posts are marked with a symbol of a telephone and an arrow, showing the direction of the nearest emergency telephone. The marker posts are now placed 100m apart. The eighth post has a double arrow which shows that the nearest telephone is half a mile in either direction.

Right:

A vehicle has broken down in a 'contraflow'. The driver has moved the vehicle partially off the carriageway, and the hazard warning lights have been switched on. The driver cannot do anything else but wait for the Police to arrive. He/she should certainly not make a foolhardy attempt to cross the carriageway to reach the emergency telephone.

Below right:

Should the vehicle break down before reaching the hard shoulder, it should, if possible, be moved off the carriageway, bearing in mind the immediate danger from passing traffic. Here the driver is trying to move the vehicle off the carriageway and on to the hard shoulder.

Far right:

Some sections of motorways do not have a hard shoulder. If a breakdown occurs on this section of the carriageway, the dangers are obvious.

Left:
This slip road has no hard shoulder, so if your vehicle breaks down here, try to move it as far on to the verge as is practicably possible.

Below left:
Should your vehicle break down, try to get as far to the left of the hard shoulder as possible. Do not leave the vehicle from the offside, but from the nearside as this driver is doing, thus keeping away from the danger of passing traffic.

Right:
Try to stop near an emergency telephone, thereby reducing the risk of potential danger from passing traffic while walking to and from a telephone. If possible, turn hazard warning lights on.

Far right:
This is the inside of an emergency telephone cabinet. Note that a hearing aid volume control is provided for those who need it. There is no dial; all you have to do is lift the handset and listen for the Police control centre, who will ask you if you have broken down. You do not need any money to contact the Police, as you have a direct line to them, regardless of the time. There is no telephone exchange involved in the line of communication.

Right:
This driver could have stopped near the telephone box but did not, and therefore has put herself in potential danger — it would have been even more dangerous in adverse weather conditions.

Far left:

The emergency telephones are provided in pairs (one on each side of the carriageway) at one-mile intervals. Should an emergency telephone not work, then you have to walk to the next one, or wait for the Police to arrive. Under no circumstances should you cross the carriageway to use another telephone.

Left:

There are numerous types of safety equipment that can be carried in a vehicle. Make sure that they are immediately available should a breakdown occur. This will reduce danger while stationary on the hard shoulder. This driver has complied with the advice given in the *Highway Code*; cones have been put out — the first 15m from the obstruction and next to the verge; the other two cones have been placed in line.

Left:

The same driver carried a red warning sign (triangle), and has placed it 150m from the obstruction. If the triangle is used, do not forget to collect it before you move off.

Right:

There is no hard and fast rule about what you and your passengers should do when waiting for assistance on the side of a motorway. The decision whether to keep passengers in the vehicle or not can only be determined by the prevailing circumstances. We have seen what action should be taken to warn other drivers of an obstruction. This driver has informed the Police that her vehicle has broken down and requested the assistance of the motoring organisation to which she belongs. She has taken refuge on the embankment while waiting for assistance to arrive. At night, or in adverse weather, an embankment is not an ideal place to be, so it would be more appropriate to sit in the vehicle; but always bear in mind the danger of traffic.

Right:

This vehicle has broken down. The driver could have made an effort to move the vehicle closer to the French drain, thereby reducing the possibility of his vehicle being struck by passing traffic. No steps have been taken to warn other drivers of the obstruction. Apart from being dangerous, he could render himself liable to prosecution.

Far right:

Should you have rectified the fault yourself, and are about to rejoin the carriageway, you should build up your speed on the hardshoulder before joining the left-hand lane, when it is safe to do so.

If you break down and you are not a member of a motoring organisation, the Police will give you two options for the removal of the obstruction from the motorway. First, you can get someone nearby to tow the vehicle away or repair it. A limited period of time will be allowed for this to be accomplished. If it is possible, the Police will make the necessary phone call on your behalf. The second option is that the Police contact a local vehicle recovery company, who will remove the obstruction from the motorway to its premises. The cost of this service will have to be paid by you. Should you have no means of paying for this service, your vehicle could be impounded by the recovery company until payment is made. Should a repair have to be carried out as well, you will have to negotiate the cost with the recovery company. Bear in mind that if you allow your vehicle to run out of fuel, one gallon of petrol could cost you as much as £50 depending on how far the recovery vehicle has had to travel to bring you fuel.

Above right:
The driver of the recovery vehicle has checked all the appropriate paperwork before any action is taken to move the vehicle. The driver of the white car has been asked by the driver of Automobile Association vehicle to sit in the passenger compartment of the recovery vehicle, thereby reducing the risk of the driver wandering about. The hazard warning lights have also been switched on.

Right:
The broken-down vehicle is being loaded on to the recovery vehicle. When safely loaded, the vehicle and passenger will be transported to the arranged destination. This service is called 'Relay', and is available to any driver when the appropriate subscription is paid, which must be before the breakdown occurs.

Obstructions

Should anything fall from your vehicle, or if you see something fall from another vehicle on to the carriageway, do not try to retrieve or move it. Use an emergency telephone to inform the Police of the danger. When you use the telephone, tell the Police what and where the danger is. When you are ready to rejoin the carriageway, drive along the hard shoulder to build your speed up. When a safe gap can be seen in the traffic in the left-hand lane, you should already be travelling at the same speed as traffic on the motorway.

Right:
Numerous items of debris have fallen from a vehicle travelling in the nearside lane, thereby causing danger to other drivers.

Below right:
Should you decide to report the danger, don't forget to use your mirrors and to indicate the move to the left.

Below:
When you report the danger, be precise about the location, otherwise there could be a delay in removing the obstruction.

4 Driving Disciplines

Overtaking

Thoughtless and inconsiderate overtaking has been the cause of numerous serious accidents. When you realise that you are catching up with another vehicle, you will have to apply 'acceleration sense'. This can only be achieved by relaxing or increasing pressure on the accelerator pedal, thereby adjusting speed to suit the circumstances. The system of Control is explained in depth in *Advanced Driving.* The following pictures show some examples of dangerous driving, committed after the decision to overtake was taken.

Below:
The driver of the white car decided to overtake the heavy goods vehicle. Without looking in his mirrors — and therefore without any knowledge of the position and speed of following vehicles — he has used his direction indicator signal and changed course, thereby forcing a passing driver to take evasive action to avoid a collision.

Right:
A driver in the left lane has got boxed in, and has decided to overtake the heavy goods vehicle, regardless of the position and speed of other traffic. He has used his indicator and if he changes course, a collision could occur.

Below right:
Should the Police see a driver commit a dangerous, thoughtless or irresponsible manoeuvre, the driver will be stopped and reported.

Far left:

Make sure it is safe to overtake before doing anything else. This can only be achieved by making effective use of mirrors. Then act sensibly on the information gained. This driver is using the offside mirror; two vehicles can be seen directly behind and another in an overtaking position. The decision to overtake cannot be made until the vehicle in the middle lane has passed when the mirrors will have to be checked again. Then if it is safe to do so, the driver will be able to overtake. If in doubt, wait.

Above left:

Don't get too close to the vehicle you intend to overtake.

Below left:

These drivers are all travelling at the same speed and have bunched together. This is dangerous and unnecessary. All that was needed was for some of the drivers to adjust their speed. They didn't, and in consequence are following too closely and in formation with each other.

Right:
CORRECT OVERTAKING PROCEDURE.
If you are travelling faster than the vehicle in front of you, you will have to decide whether to overtake or slow down.

Far right:
If you decide to overtake, the first thing to do is look in your mirror(s), so that you know the speed and distance of any following traffic.

Below right:
When it is safe to do so, and if required, signal your intention to move out by using the direction indicator signal. Remember that a signal gives you no right of way or protection whatsoever: it is a signal of intent and no more.

Left:
When you are sure it is safe to do so, steer a steady course to a position to overtake the vehicle in front.

Below left:
A vehicle travelling alongside another vehicle is in a zone of danger. Don't stay there too long! Overtaking should be completed as quickly as possible, subject to the prevailing traffic and weather conditions at the time. Always exercise patience and leave a margin of safety for errors that can be made by the driver in front who may not be aware that he/she is being overtaken.

Right:

To make sure it is safe to return to the left lane, the mirror(s) must be used.

Far right:

When you can see the vehicle that has been overtaken in the mirror, signal your intention to move to the left by using the direction indicator signal.

Below right:

You should steer a steady course to the left lane. Do not cut in on the vehicle you have just overtaken.

Following Distance

Nose to tail collisions should never occur, but they do. After the accident, the excuses or reasons why the collision happened are offered in abundance. 'Why did you brake so hard?' 'The road surface must have been slippery.' 'Your stop-light signals don't work.' 'The rear of your car came towards me.'

The real reason for the accident will in all probability never be admitted, but the evidence of the damage sustained will show who has been at fault.

It takes the average driver 0.7sec to respond to a sudden situation. In that time the distance travelled would be 30.8ft for a vehicle travelling at 30mph. There are pictures in this book where vehicles are travelling far in excess of the 30mph, with less that 30.8ft between them. What logical reason for doing this can be given by these drivers?

If instead they allowed sufficient time for their journey, instead of treating the carriageway as a 'rat run', and concentrated on their driving, instead of using their vehicle as the means of travelling from 'A' to 'B' as quickly as possible, then a major contribution would be made towards making motorways safer to use.

Far left, bottom:
When you see this sign, take heed of the advice.

Left:
Some drivers think that by following a vehicle closely they will save fuel by using the slipstream. The only cheap drive this will get you is the one to the morgue.

Below left:
MARGIN OF SAFETY.
When following another vehicle, you should allow at least one metre for each mph of your speed, therefore if you are travelling at 30mph you should have at least 30m between you and the vehicle in front. At 60mph there should be a 60m gap; if the road surface is wet the gap should be doubled. Should an overtaking vehicle pull into the gap in front of you, look in the mirrors and, if safe to do so, reduce speed slightly, thereby regaining your margin of safety.

Right:
The speed limit in this 'contraflow' is 50mph. Some drivers are not even allowing 50ft separation distance.

THINKING DISTANCE at 30 M.P.H.

Distance travelled during reaction time

Time(sec.)	Distance (ft.)	Time(sec.)	Distance (ft.)
·175	7·7	·475	20·9
·2	8·8	·5	22
·225	9·9	·525	23·1
·25	11	·55	24·2
·275	12·1	·575	25·3
·3	13·2	·6	26·4
·325	14·3	·625	27·5
·35	15·4	·65	28·6
·375	16·5	·675	29·7
·4	17·6	·7	30·8
·425	18·7	·725	31·9
·45	19·8	·75	33

REMEMBER—This does not include braking distance which at 30m.p.h is a further 45ft.

TOTAL STOPPING DISTANCE

Distance travelled assuming an about average reaction time

M.P.H	Reaction Distance	Braking Distance	Total Stopping Distance
	ft.	ft.	ft.
20	20	20	40
30	30	45	75
40	40	80	120
50	50	125	175
60	60	180	240
70	70	245	315

REMEMBER—These braking distances only apply on dry road surfaces. On wet roads, they could double.

Far left, top:
This table shows reaction times and the distance covered while you decide whether to apply the brake.

Far left, bottom:
This table shows the actual distance being travelled prior to stopping.

Left:
This is a novel approach to spacing problems. White chevrons have been painted on the road, 3m in length and every 40m. If the advice is taken, a driver will be travelling 80m from the vehicle in front.

Below left:
This aerial view of the chevrons on the carriageway shows what an excellent margin of safety can be obtained. The idea has been adopted from the French, who have used them for a number of years.

Lane Discipline

Regardless of how many lanes there are on a motorway, you should always keep to the left. The only exceptions to this rule are illustrated in this section.

Bad lane discipline is one of the main causes of traffic congestion on motorways and can be extremely dangerous. Some drivers try to enforce the national speed limit, by driving at 70mph and not letting other cars past. This too is potentially dangerous.

Then there are the members of 'I always drive in the middle lane' club, when the left-hand lane is clear of traffic. This selfish and dangerous attitude is taken by people who are probably unaware that they are blocking the path of heavy goods vehicles which cannot overtake in the lane nearest to the central reserve.

Another type of dangerous driver seems to think the carriageway and hard shoulder are a free for all. Overtaking is carried out on the left of other traffic including the hard shoulder, in a desperate effort to pass slower moving or stationary vehicles regardless of safety. Driving cars at speed is dangerous. It is made more dangerous by bad drivers. Safety is more important than speed.

Left:
At some junctions the number of lanes will be reduced and, if you intend to continue on the motorway, you will have to change lane to the middle lane, which in all probability will become the nearside lane after the junction has been passed.

Above:
When approaching roadworks, it is of the utmost importance that you stay in the lane you are in. (See Roadworks in Chapter 5.)

Right:
Should you be in congested traffic, do not get impatient and – like the people here – drive on the hard shoulder to jump the queue. This is illegal and dangerous and it blocks an emergency route to an accident (possibly the cause of the traffic congestion). If you are caught driving on the hard shoulder, you could be summonsed.

Right:
**FOG
When you see fog, switch on the headlights (with the beam dipped). You must not use your rear fog lamps unless visibility is seriously reduced — that is, generally, reduced to a distance of less than 100m. Do not use them simply because it is dark or raining. Make sure too that you check your mirrors, so that you know where other vehicles are and how fast they are going.**

Below right:
Keep a safe distance from the vehicle in front, so that you and other road users have the time and distance to pull up. It cannot be stressed too strongly that this is what will keep you out of trouble and avoid large 'concertina' accidents. Always be ready and able to brake to a standstill in the distance visible ahead of you.

Far right:
Some drivers rely on warning lights to inform them of danger rather than using their eyes to see it. To assist drivers who are unable to recognise fog, fog detectors are being installed on many motorways (see 209A). When visibility falls below 300m, they automatically switch on matrix signals to display the legend 'Fog'.

Adverse Weather

You should always make allowances for the mistakes of other drivers. It is unsafe to assume that another driver will react correctly to any given situation; he may have passed the driving test only that day, or may be driving a strange or defective vehicle. They may be naturally aggressive or thoughtless, or attempting to drive beyond their capabilities for the prevailing conditions in order to keep an urgent appointment.

It is surprising — but true — that most drivers are unaware of one essential fact: you should always be in a position to stop your vehicle well within the distance that can be seen to be clear ahead. Horrific pile-ups in mist, fog and smoke prove that this rule has not been applied. Above all, you must concentrate on what is going on around you, observe the road and plan ahead. This is particularly true in adverse weather conditions.

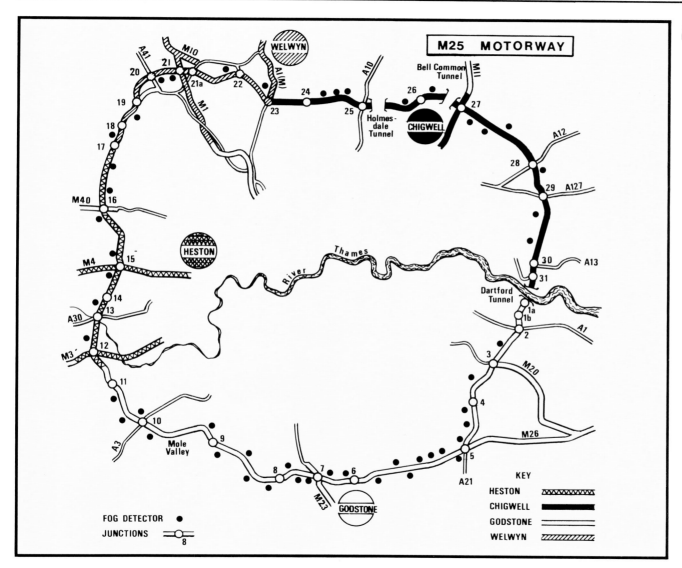

Left:
Fog detectors on the M25.

Right:

Once the fog detectors have activated the matrix signs, you must comply with the temporary maximum speed restriction. No doubt there will be at least one driver, who will think the information given by the matrix signs is a waste of time. Look out for this driver, he could be behind you!

Far right:

HEAVY RAIN.
When driving on stretches of road affected by heavy rain, a curtain of spray from other vehicles will reduce further a driver's view of the road ahead. In such conditions you must use your headlamps with the beam dipped, thereby informing other road users of your presence.

Right:

HIGH WINDS.
The road situation can change at any time — for example, a high-sided vehicle could be affected by cross-wind, or could pull out to overtake. Always be vigilant and watch out for strong winds. Look at the tops of trees in the distance, and you will get an idea of the force of the wind.

Above right:

SNOW AND ICE.
A good driver is one who looks well ahead, recognises any change in road surface conditions, and applies the correct values of braking, acceleration and steering. In this photograph the lane that the lorry is in should be used, and the potentially dangerous snow-covered lane avoided. Adverse weather conditions, no matter what the cause, may demand a drastic reduction in speed to keep within the bounds of safety. Where ice is present, four times the normal stopping distance must be allowed, and so your distance from the vehicle in front must be extended to allow for the extra distance for stopping.

Crawler Lanes

Left:
When a motorway runs through hilly country an extra lane may be provided, if heavy commercial vehicles form a substantial proportion of traffic. This extra lane is sometimes called a 'Crawler' lane, its purpose is to siphon off slow-moving commercial vehicles allowing space for faster vehicles to overtake.

As a guide, an extra lane may be provided on uphill grades of 3% (1 in 33) over 1,500ft in length, and on a 4% (1 in 25) grade over 1,000ft long. Where possible, the two carriageways are graduated, to provide a less steep gradient for heavy goods vehicles, thus avoiding the need for a crawler lane.

Road markings and signs tell drivers that a crawler lane is provided. Should the lane be clear of heavy goods vehicles, you can use it as a left-hand lane.

Left:
This sign warns drivers that there is no crawler lane. This means that slow-moving heavy goods vehicles could be in the lane in front of you. So slow down!

Right:

A crawler lane being used. The sign also warns drivers that it ends 800yd ahead. You should now check your mirrors so that you know the position and speed of following traffic and can start to plan your movement into the next lane.

Below right:

This sign informs drivers that the crawler lane ends 400yd ahead. At this distance, a driver should be moving into the next lane to the right — providing it is safe to do so.

Left:
A white warning arrow painted on the carriageway shows a driver that a change of course should have been made. If you have not changed course by the time the arrow is reached, you could have put yourself and others in a dangerous situation.

Below left:
Should you still be in the crawler lane by the time you reach this sign, give way to any traffic in the lane on the immediate right. Always plan your driving well ahead and take appropriate action well before reaching a hazard.

Right:

The driver of the white van and the traffic immediately in front of it are staying in the crawler lane to its end, which can be dangerous.

Below right:

When a motorway runs through hilly country, it may have been possible to construct the carriageways at different levels, thereby providing a less steep gradient for heavy goods vehicles. This obviates the need for a crawler lane.

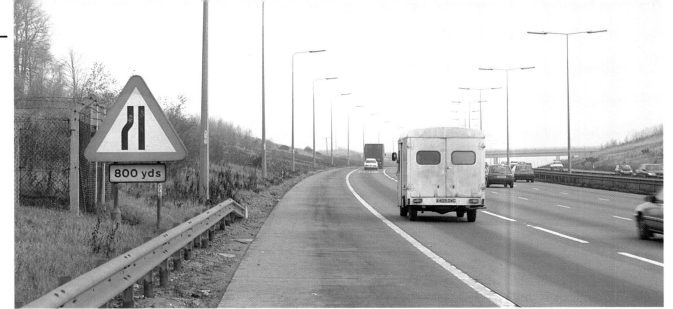

5 Maintenance and Services

Below:
Before a major set of roadworks starts, warning signs will appear to enable drivers to plan alternative routes.

Roadworks

However well a motorway has been constructed, there will come a time when resurfacing or major repairs will be required. As motorways were constructed in lengthy sections, it follows that repairs could be extended for several miles with consequent traffic restrictions. Bear this in mind if you intend to use the motorway while repairs are being carried out.

Roadworks must be planned carefully, not only to minimise the risk of accidents to the workmen and to users of the motorway, but also to complete the work in the shortest possible time. As a last resort, one side of the carriageway will have to be closed. In such an event, traffic from one side of the motorway will be diverted through the emergency crossing point in the central reserve to the opposite side of the carriageway; this is called a 'contraflow'. Every precaution should be taken when travelling in what has become a two-way traffic system. Any temporary, mandatory or advisory speed limit should be complied with. The following sequence of pictures illustrates what you will see as you approach and negotiate roadworks.

Right:

The first notification of roadworks is seen on a warning sign.

Below right:

The next warning sign shows the distance from the roadworks plus other information.

Far right:

The third warning sign informs a driver that the roadworks are one mile ahead. By looking well ahead you should be able to see their start.

Don't take the message on this sign for granted. Check your mirrors and speedometer so that you know the speed and position of your own and other vehicles. A reduction in speed should also be considered now.

Below left:
When you see this sign, it is important that you get into the appropriate lane for your intended direction of travel. Should you have to change course, use your mirrors and signal accordingly. There is only three-quarters of a mile left to get into the required lane before the lane restrictions.

Right:

Should a vehicle break down between this sign and the end of the roadworks, it will be moved free of charge to a vehicle breakdown recovery compound. The cost of storage/repair will have to be negotiated between the driver and the vehicle recovery company. The main objective is to clear any obstruction from the carriageway.

Below right:

Now you have a quarter of a mile before reaching the lane restrictions.

Left:
You can see people ignoring the compulsory speed limit at every roadworks. To some drivers reducing speed to comply with the traffic sign is inconvenient, regardless of the danger created. At some roadworks the Police use radar to check the speed of vehicles. Comply with the order given by the traffic signs, it could save your life.

Far left, bottom:
This traffic sign warns you that a deviation in course to the left will have to be made 200yd ahead. The mirrors should be used, and a reduction in speed considered, bearing in mind that the maximum speed limit is 50mph.

Below left:
The hard shoulder is about to be used as the nearside lane.

Right:

A driver who intends to leave the motorway at junction 9 should be in the left-hand lane. Drivers who are in the offside lane will be diverted into a contraflow traffic system. Once in the system a driver MUST NOT for any reason overtake any vehicle. This is one situation when common sense must prevail.

Centre right:

This sign confirms the message given by the previous sign; it also reminds drivers that there is a speed limit in operation.

Below right:

This sign warns you that a lane diversion is 50yd ahead. Check your mirrors, so that you know the position and speed of any following traffic.

Far right:

This aerial view of a working contraflow shows the danger being created by drivers following too close to each other, allowing no margin for safety.

Above:

This sign informs you that there is a junction 200yd ahead. If you intend to leave the motorway, use the mirrors, signal your intention to do so, and consider reducing speed.

Above right:

This is junction 9 to which the previous signs referred. The traffic signs in the central reserve tell you that there is still a speed limit in operation, and the end of the contraflow is 50yd ahead. Traffic will be redirected back to the left-hand side of the central reserve.

Right:

At the end of the roadworks, a driver will see the signs displayed here. The mirrors should be used and speed should not be increased until the national speed limit sign has been passed and it is safe to do so.

Motorway Maintenance

To achieve a good standard of maintenance and tidiness on motorways, the county council acts as agent for the Department of Transport for the maintenance of the stretches of motorway that pass through its county. To achieve this objective, it is necessary to have motorway maintenance compounds either alongside the motorway or next to a service area. Today's policy is to site the compound off the motorway, but near to a junction, thereby increasing the options of access.

Far left, top:
This maintenance compound is situated near a junction, thus given two options of access to the motorway.

Far left, bottom:
Numerous types of debris are found on motorways. Pieces of a tyre can be seen here on the hard shoulder, thereby creating potential danger.

Left:
This propeller shaft was found on the verge next to the hard shoulder. The driver of the vehicle it came from is probably still wondering why he came to a stop.

Right:

Motorways are inspected regularly to remove dangerous debris. The crew of this motorway maintenance vehicle have just removed something from the carriageway.

Below right:

The maintenance of motorways is not as simple as one might imagine, especially where there are grassed areas which are an expensive problem during the spring and summer. Grass on the central reserve looks untidy if not properly maintained, as seen here. These days the whole reservation would be covered in tarmac.

Diversions

Sometimes it is necessary to close a section of a motorway to traffic because of an emergency. When this happens special signs may be displayed to advise drivers already on the motorway, or intending to join it, of an alternative route. If this happens, follow them and you will rejoin the motorway past the point of closure. If the diversion route is simple to identify, it will be indicated on the special signs by reference to its route classification number. There will be no extra or special signs along the route. However, where the alternative route is complex, it may be indicated by the use of a special symbol — for example, a rectangle, diamond, triangle or circle — which is either attached to existing direction signs or displayed separately. Drivers diverted from a closed section of motorway will be advised to follow a specific symbol along the diversion route until the motorway is rejoined or they see signs indicating the direction back to the motorway. In some areas, all-black symbols are used. To assist you further, a booklet prepared by the Department of Transport titled *Know your traffic signs* is available from any HMSO publications centre and all good bookshops.

Below:
This sign informs a driver that the symbol of a diamond identifies the route that should be followed.

Right:

Once off the motorway, the symbol of a diamond can be seen on a primary traffic route sign. Continue on your journey following the symbol.

Far right:

Unfortunately at times the identification symbol can lead to confusion: this sign shows two symbols, a rectangle and a triangle.

Below right:

This sign also directs drivers to Cambridge, with the symbols of a square and triangle, but no rectangle.

Service Areas

On some motorways, 24hr service areas are provided with adequate parking for private and commercial users. The services available include fuel, a cafeteria or restaurant and toilet facilities; some service areas have emergency repair facilities and overnight accommodation. Should you be considering a long journey, you are advised to plan regular stops at 2hr intervals, not only to give your vehicle a rest but yourself as well.

Below left:
This sign shows the name of the company that runs the service area, and the services being offered, plus the cost of one litre of petrol.

5 Maintenance and Services

Right:

The message on the sign is self-explanatory, but many drivers ignore the advice, and approach the service area too fast.

Below right:

Lorries and coaches have to use the hard shoulder to reach this service area, so if a vehicle has broken down, you will have to change lane. Make sure you check your mirrors and that it is safe to pass the obstruction before you attempt to do so.

Right:

When leaving a service area, don't take it for granted that a one-way traffic system is in operation. This traffic sign informs a driver that he could encounter oncoming traffic.

The Police

Many schemes and regulations have been introduced since the first motorway was opened to try to reduce the number of accidents. The most consistently successful has been the continued presence of Police motor patrols, which supervise the behaviour and advise other road users. Their overseeing of traffic maintains a smooth and safe flow of vehicles.

Motorway Police patrols have specialist vehicles and highly trained personnel; they deal with all emergency calls received by the information room and anyone else who needs their assistance. The Police patrols endeavour to enforce lane discipline by example, or verbal warning. If a serious offence has been committed the driver could be prosecuted.

Below:
Observation cameras are deployed at intersections and other busy sections of carriageway.

Right:
This panel of screens is in the control/information room. Numerous sections of the motorway can be seen on the screens.

Far right:
Should the Police request you to pull up on the hard shoulder for any reason, they will do so by the use of blue flashing lights and/or headlamps.

Below right:
The officer is explaining why he has stopped the driver.

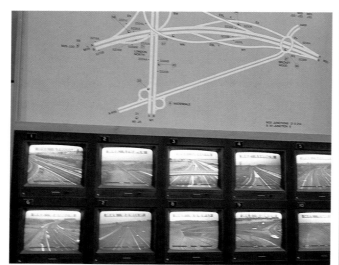

Left:
This gives an idea of the sort of danger that some people create. There has just been an accident. The drivers and their passengers are seen discussing the situation while standing on the carriageway, while traffic is passing.

Below left:
When the Police arrive at the scene, the pedestrians and damaged vehicles are removed from the carriageway.

6 Leaving a Motorway

Leaving a motorway can be as dangerous as joining one. You should know well in advance which exit you want to use and position the vehicle for leaving the motorway in good time. Don't be like some inconsiderate drivers who have no driving plan and realise at the last moment that the next exit is the one to be taken. In consequence, they cut across two or more lanes, with no concern of the speed or position of other traffic.

Bottom left:
Wait until you are on the slip road before reducing speed. Some slip roads have a sharp bend, so make sure you reduce your speed before reaching the bend, particularly when the road surface is wet. This driver is in the correct position in the slip lane, travelling at the correct speed, and using the correct signal, which is about to be cancelled, so as not to confuse another road user on the approach to the roundabout ahead. Check the speedometer and adjust your speed accordingly, bearing in mind that on leaving a motorway speed can be very deceptive.

Experience in driving a motor vehicle cannot be bought, it has to be earned by driving many thousands of miles under all conditions. This book illustrates the sort of information and knowledge needed to drive safely on motorways.

It is a sad fact of life that too many fatal accidents happen on motorways, and a large proportion of the blame must be laid at the door of the people who use the roads without due care and attention. Lack of concentration and planning can be a matter of life and death — it could be yours or somebody else's. Think about it.

Below:
Hogging the overtaking lane is a multi-national problem. This Austrian poster shows just that! Keep in the inside lane unless overtaking.

Safety Summary

Speed

Don't speed! The national speed limit on British motorways is 70mph. It's better to be safe than late!

Stopping Distance

At 60mph your car is travelling at 88 feet per second. Your stopping distance is 240 feet on a dry road. You should always be able to stop in the space you can see in front of you. What if the car in front has a mechanical failure or a tyre blows out? Will you be able to stop before you hit it?

Mirrors

Use your mirrors! You don't have eyes in the back of your head, but mirrors are the next best thing. You must be aware of what is behind and on either side of you.

Overtaking

Plan your overtaking well in advance. Don't just pull out. Before you decide to overtake make sure it's safe to do so and consider why you are overtaking. Do you need to?

Lane Discipline

Keep in the left-hand lane unless overtaking. Remember the Highway Code advice. Don't block the path of other road users.

Observation

Look well ahead. Concentration and road observation are the most important factors in safer motorway driving. Look well ahead of the vehicle in front and you'll see stop lights early giving you more time to react.